# ENTREPRENEUR'S HEART
## A VISIONARY'S JOURNAL

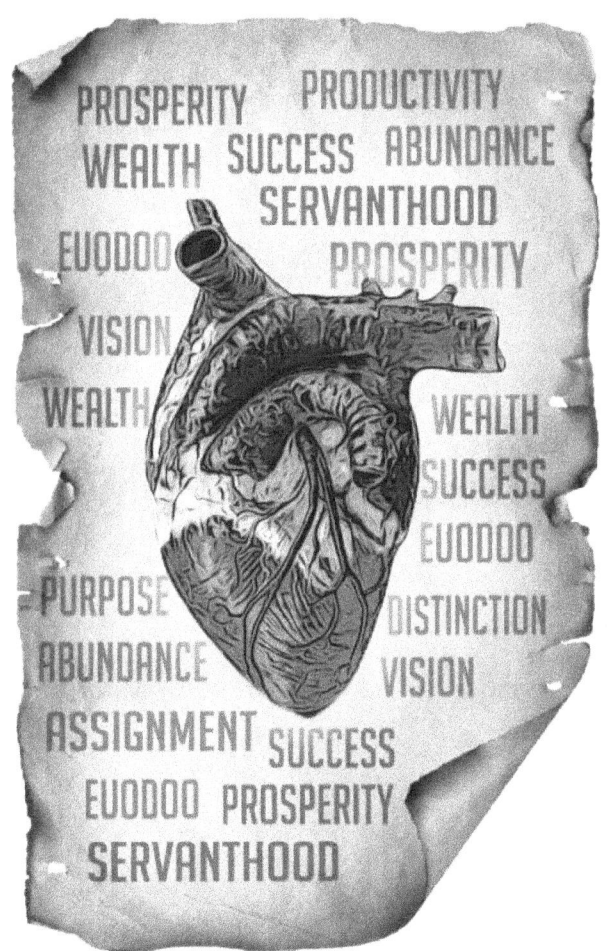

# AMANDA LATRICE

# ENTREPRENEUR'S HEART
### A Visionary's JOURNAL

This Journal Belongs to:

_____

## Amanda Latrice, Visionary

Amanda Latrice is the founder and visionary of Euodoo Enterprises which was launched in August 2015. In December of 2008 she became burdened by lack of understanding surrounding finances and business strategy that was happening in business, ministries, and households and wanted to educate individuals, business, and communities on how to effectively budget, govern, and understand their finances and the internal structures of business.

Amanda is a strategist and is an upcoming leader in her generation in the area of business. She graduated from Ball State University in 2010 with a Bachelor's Degree in Accounting and a minor in American Sign Language. In August of 2015 she graduated from Indiana Wesleyan University with a Master's in Business Administration and a concentration in applied management. She has been working and volunteering in Human Resources, Administration, and Accounting since she was in high school and has become trained in system integrations, implementations, policy and procedures, and internal structural development in each position she has carried.

She is a member of Kingdom Shifters Christian Empowerment Center in Muncie, IN where she serves as an administrator, an elder, and member of the intercessory team. She is also the administrator of Kingdom Wellness Counseling and Mentoring Center, and Kingdom Shifters Ministries, where she brings strategy and structure with a kingdom mindset accompanied with a business perspective. She has helped to establish dance ministries, orchestrate conferences and ministry events, and has traveled in ministry consistently, while ministering in the areas of dance, prayer, spiritual warfare, and deliverance. Amanda has a prophetic mantle which encompasses a strong deliverance and healing anointing. Additionally, Amanda possess the gift of administration, dance, teaching, and all manner of prayer. She also carries the mantle of wealth which drives her passion to see the Kingdom of God impact the market place. Amanda has such a heart and a passion to see individuals, businesses, communities, and ministries succeed and take on a business mindset with a perspective that will impact their communities and generations to come.

## Entrepreneur's Heart: A Visionary's Journal

*"Entrepreneur's Heart: A Visionary's Journal"* is designed to assist visionaries in writing out their business ideas in an organized manner that can be turned into a business plan.

euodooenterprises12@gmail.com

euodooenterprises.com

Connect with Amanda Latrice via Facebook or YouTube

Copyright 2018 – Euodoo Enterprises, LLC. All rights reserved.

Images are either copyright free, public domain images or used with permission of the graphic artist.

This book is protected by the copyright laws of the United States of America. This book may not be reprinted for commercial gain or profit. The use of occasional page copying for personal or group study is permitted and encouraged. Permission will be granted with written request.

# Entrepreneur's Heart
## *A Visionary's  JOURNAL*

*This Journal is designed to assist visionaries in writing out their business ideas in a manner that can be turned into a business plan when the time comes. Each journal section will have a question to prompt study and further assist you in bring definition to the idea you have. As entrepreneurs there are times where an idea will come to you and you don't have time to figure out what section or prompt to turn to.  In this journal you will also have a section that will be available to simply jot down thoughts and ideas that may come quick and fast.*

**My hope is that as you continue to write and study, that clarity and definition to the business idea you have will be given.**

*Love and Blessings,*
*- Amanda Latrice*

# *Entrepreneur's Establishment*

The name of your company has a meaning and will be what the first thing that establishes your brand. Let your name really reflect the focus of the business, ministry, or community event and the goals and purpose for which it is being developed.

Your company name is an establishment of its purpose in the earth.

*What is are some names you are considering for your business? What is the meaning of each name?*

*How do the names you listed reflect your business idea?*

# Entrepreneur's Purpose

*Visionaries are the solution to a problem. We recognize that there is a need and we put action to creating the solution. We listen to the hearts of the people in the region as well as the region itself and we create and establish a clear vison that shifts they way customers/consumers view that particular situation.*

*What problem do you see your vision being the solution for?*

# *Mission Possible*

*As a visionary it is important to know what your core values are, your purpose, and what makes you do what you do. These items will help you keep a clear focus in the mist of distractions and various changes that may occur in the economy, in your region, or in your personal life.*

*What are your core values?*

# What is your purpose in developing this vision?

*What are the reasons you want to do this every day?*

# Clear Vision

*Clear Vision gives you the why and how for implementing the mission (purpose and assignment of the business idea). It gives you and those who will connect with you clarity on the purpose and how they can assist.*

*How does your vision help people?*

## *What is your business trying to achieve?*

*How are you planning to achieve it?*

# *Start it up and Shift*

*Establishing a vision does cost and does have sacrifices, but when you know the purpose for which you ae doing it, your drive and focus becomes only to produce and reproduce your assignment.*

*Strategically understanding and laying out what cost you might incur before the business ever takes off is important so that you know what you may need to budget and be prepared for in the development stage of your business.*

*Do you manage inventory? What kind?*

*Look up pricing of your inventory and determine realistically as you start how much you would like to keep on hand.*

*Look up vendors that will allow you to purchase wholesale. What is the minimum amount you can purchase?*

*List Vendors you would consider purchasing from.*

# List other start up cost that may be incurred?
*(i.e. workshops, trainings, licensing, and CEU's)*

# *What people are looking for you?*

*Each entrepreneur has a demographic that they are assigned to. Knowing the group of customers and clients that are in need of your business is key to being able to draw the right person and/or group.*

*Describe each group you are assigned to and why?*

*In the groups you have listed research details about each one. List how many people are in each group and how large the total market for your industry is.*

_____
_____
_____
_____
_____
_____
_____
_____
_____
_____
_____
_____
_____
_____
_____
_____

# *Uniquely you*

*There are many businesses that are within the industry that you are trying to enter into. It is important to be uniquely you and recognize your asset in the market.*

*What makes your business different than the others in your industry?*

# *Getting the Word Out*

*Knowing your audience is key to learning exactly what will work to get the word out? It will also assist in what is needed in reference to content, technology, and location.*

*It allows you to form a brand that will reach those you are targeting.*

*What ways does your target audience receive their information?*

*What kind of ads does your audience respond to?*

## *What software/technology might you need to reach your target audience?*

# *Support*

*Businesses are not one man shows. We all need people that can come along side us and assist us in executing the business to its full potential. Knowing your team and how to utilize them in your business will position them and you to walk in purpose and destiny.*

## *List team members and what area you think they would be a good fit in?*

*Process this with an open heart and mind. Do not create the list based on your wants and desires.* The very ones you would never have thought of may be the best ones to help you with your business.

*List and describe any mentors, investors, former professors etc.. That can help you as a business owner?*

# Business Thoughts

*List business ideas and strategies as they come to you.*

_____
_____
_____
_____
_____
_____
_____
_____
_____
_____
_____
_____
_____
_____
_____
_____
_____
_____
_____
_____
_____

# *Resources*

## For more resources check out

*www.kingdomshiftingbooks.com*
*www.euodooenterprises.com*
*www.kingdomshifters.com*
*www.kswu.net*
*www.amazon.com*

www.ingramcontent.com/pod-product-compliance
Lightning Source LLC
Chambersburg PA
CBHW070815220526
45466CB00002B/666